RAINBOW

A First Book of Pride

by Michael Genhart, PhD

illustrated by Anne Passchier

Magination Press • Washington, DC
American Psychological Association

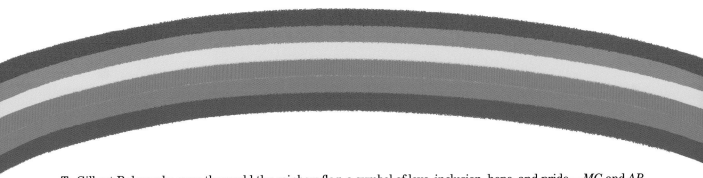

To Gilbert Baker, who gave the world the rainbow flag, a symbol of love, inclusion, hope, and pride—*MG* and *AP*

Books for Kids From the
American Psychological Association

Magination Press is a registered trademark of the
American Psychological Association. Order books at
maginationpress.org.

Cataloging-in-Publication data is on file at the
Library of Congress.

ISBN-13: 978-1-4338-3087-7 (hardcover)

Manufactured in the United States of America
10 9 8 7 6 5 4

Rainbows!

Every color means something.

Red means life.

Orange is healing.

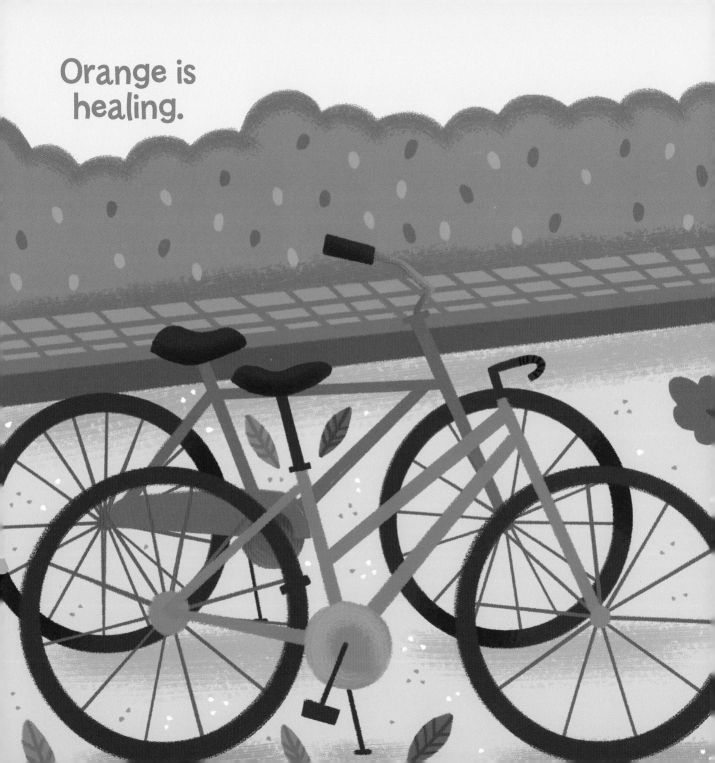

Yellow is sunlight.

Green is nature.

Blue is harmony.

Violet is spirit.

Rainbows make the world smile.

Rainbows sing out.

Be happy. Be love. Be proud.

Rainbows are so colorful and beautiful, nature's way of smiling at us all. Rainbow flags are happy too. They celebrate love, hope, diversity, and acceptance. Waving the flag says, "This is who I am, and I stand proud!" Happy Pride!

Love, your rainbow friend,
Michael